Domesticity

Jennifer Anne Moses

ISBN- 978-1-7374758-5-9
Library of Congress Control Number: 2022949441

Published by:

Blue Jade Press, LLC

Blue Jade Press, LLC
Vineland, NJ 08360
www.bluejadepress.com

In loving memory of my mother, Carol Whitehill Moses

Table of Contents

The Sixties

Our Kennedy was a girl
Blond, freckled, blue-eyed.
Well—they all were.

We vied for her attention on the play-ground
the hard black top
with swings and a seesaw, the whirl-around.

Fierce and determined, scabby-kneed
Her white flash of white underpants—
Heedless of blood, her speed—

The rest of us lacked
a quality, a glamour, a heedless going forth
it was—a fact.

Spilling from trees, diving off banisters,
The New Frontier, Civil Rights—
hounds, rabbits, hamsters.

In the middle of that pack of–was it eleven?
They jumped off rooftops and from high branches of high trees,
an upward thrusted middle finger towards heaven.

Then heaven called out: I've had it! Enough!
1968 sizzled with corrupted hope
In the third grade we dealt in fisticuff.

Mrs. O'Neille came to school in dark sunglasses
she was ashamed of her red-rimmed eyes
from crying, keening—the casket, the ashes.

The assassin: a new word, like a sore:
Sirhan Sirhan—is that a name?
His blue black blood on the concrete floor.

Our Kennedy, when she at last returned to school
was quiet, almost cowed, almost demure—
and then she burst forth, a broken blazing jewel.

Planning the Garden

In the siege of March
Plan the garden
That patch of mud where the dogs
Ran wild
Tearing up roots
Scattering flower heads
And petals.
Plan to plant daffodils
Or no:
Something more wild,
More wildly American:
Rag weed, Joe pie; yellow-topped terrors
For the yapping next door dog to fight
In his terrified running doggy dreams.

That spot behind the stumped shrubs
Where the neighbor's weed tree overhangs
With its deprivation of sunlight
Also needs tuning.
First the pruning of the neighbor's invasively
Curious growth
A quick whack with pruning sheers
To quell your fears as the raging rage surges
In nearby towns
The sounds of fear.

Further still:
The spot by the well
The old unused well, long gone dry
Where dust and dirt collect and cry
Out to be turned to rich brown wormy loam:
A tomb, a home—or
A patch, perhaps, of myrtle
Star of Bethlehem
Daphne Adora.

I pour over seed catalogues
Collecting colors and shine
The dazzle of paint
The rant of little Saint
Theresa, the saint of flowers.

Like me, she was drawn to gardens
To wild abundance of purple and pink
Of butterflies—birds! —the lure of ink
Inside is nothing in compare
With all that daring air
Of green and blue
Out there—

The Sunshine State

My husband of three decades
And I—
Fly to Florida
A celebration:
My uncle turns ninety.

He and his second wife
Retired there—
They play golf—
She picks at him
There's no winning with her—
His first wife, my aunt,
My late mother's late sister–

It was a big mess.

She died in distress
My poor aunt
Aware,
In her last late illness
That she ruined her life
And his
On a dare.

There was nothing there.

My cousins and I
All of us on the brink and brush of our own
Finitude
Laugh at old jokes
Tell old stories
All the horrors of our parallel youths
All those–
Untruths.

But in the bright blue azure haze
Of a bleak hot February
With its forced and brutal gaze
Old men with bitter tans
Wearing lollipop colors
And shorts, like little boys
Shirts without collars—

Stare.

The women have faces sewn into a purse.
But at least, God willing—
They're happy
They're well
The mild weather is magic
A balm—

Everything quiet and calm.

Calm, calm the non-rhythm of
The non-changing week
Cancels out the sick
And those who seek
To reach for heaven
To meet God at last
(or maybe not God,
maybe just one of his reps)
But not so fast
Not yet, not yet—
The fast big-engine big-guzzling cars speed
And all the filth and all the wealth
Hide behind thick walls made of
Sticky stealth
And the grasses burn
And the ocean is raped
And addicts find fixes—

For their escape
From the ugliness and horrors and scars we make
For the sake of—

Thoughts and prayers.
Facebook shares.

While behind those high white thick white walls
Rich white men hit small white balls.

The Crab

My mother's body
Was something I didn't want to see
Her smallish breasts with their dark brown endings
Shrunken, no-longer pink
For how her nipples dimpled inwards

Body natural
Body just because—
She had nothing to hide

We had doors but no locks
Windows but no curtains

My mother:
And her strong slim body
The body she had
Before I was born
Before she was
Floored with childbirth
The squall.
Teenagers
Resorcinol

She read—
Psychology books
Books on how to—

A section of the den
Given over to them

Ah! Her poor dear body:

Last night I dreamed
That she stripped off her top
In the car
And her breasts
Just dangled there

Terrible, like bruises
I averted my eyes

Every year on her *yartzeit,*
At break of light
My father visits her grave
Grave under winter skies—

He talks to her, he looks at the dead winter grass
Perhaps he thinks about his own
Upcoming endless non-resting rest
Until then,
The fight
Fight on!
Fight to live and not to die and while I survive
Please God
Let me be alive.

The First Wife

Hers was the larger gift
Gilded swollen red
In their heady golden bed
There was nothing she couldn't do

So she made a fool of you
In turn you turned her world all blue
Blue the smoke, the pillows, the view
She popped blood and babies and pills too

Too numerous to name a few
You lost her then and then lost two
Batshit crazy, très cuckoo

Or so they mused
Regarding you
Her very own malevolent Jew

She scooped your parings, your hair-dust, your lungs
When with
Those enticing entrancing *en* words
You dangled
Whey and curds
Domesticated herds of
Sheep and goats
Castles, moats,
Your British Isles phantasma
Deep growling vowels on television

And that terrible, endless, enduring gash

Glasgow

Big looming gloomy
Victorian buildings
Made solid with sand-stone
Red and glowing in afternoon light
When there was light

We arrived in July
For sixty, seventy days
in a row
rain fell—

I walked back and forth
Through the Botanical gardens
In the fall, the smell of fall,
Bright and damp, both–
To collect my children
From the small private school
Where they were studying insects

My nose dripped in the rain
My eyes, without lashes, dripped tears
Though I was not crying

The Journey

From inside the capsule
The towns shaped like crosses
The spackled red sparkles
Downtown at night
And in all the black softness
That spreading dark blankness
You wonder who lives there
And what do they do.

The green and red sparkling
Of earnest dead highways
The webbing of highway
The tangle of tar
Its sticky black oozing
Upon the republic
The oozing of dying
The death of the heart.

The jutting winged creature
Is just out your portal
Its wingtip all jaunty
Afloat and alight
While the night lies so smoothly
So soft and so darkly
And your neighbor nods sagely
His eyes on his screen.

Excuse me dear neighbor
What is it you're seeking
We're seeking the same thing
In the wonder of night
Of swift flying flagrantly
Over and over
the land—
Far below us and
God, how he mourns.

Homemaking

I like the domestic realm
I like making beds
Making things quick and neat
Shoes lined up, and feet
Clean
Dogs' paw wiped at the door
The floor
Swept, the sheen
Of polished wood

Outside my windows
The neighborhood
Quiet in the morning
A few cars passing by
The street—
Tarred, shiny in rain
Drizzle again
Slow gray February—
All paused before the turning

Of and when

A tender tendril, an aerie—
Comes around
Like Eflurane

Mommy

By my age you were eaten by worms

My own little mommy
Gone.
She dined on me nightly
(Me in my nighty)
(She with her fork)

And such suffering, all that suffering—
Cancer eating her like she ate me
Don't you get it? Don't you see?

In the Turning

I was a lonely child
I loved the red bud trees
When they bloomed
They were purple–not red at all
As they furred and furled the boughs
Along the lane
Where we lived

I wanted that beauty
I mourned its yearly passing

I was seventeen when our neighbor
Jack drove up in his
Cadillac
The one with an interior
Of teddy bear blue

And he, with his red face
and glass of vodka
and Camel cigarettes
(and endless regret)
Stopped, unrolled the window
and with a stricken face turned towards me
How he cried.

I was in college when he died

of cancer: chain-smoking
Isn't good for your lungs.
Or was it the booze?
Excuse me, I should remember
I loved him so—in that fleeting, teenage way

His newspaper (he had one) churned out the news
From far away, other despairs, other wars
Not ours

But we were destined to live—if not forever
Then at least until the last endeavor
Floating in the atmosphere
As we aged in a distant mirror

Acne

Small white blots
Filth on my face
Surely I'm too old for this
Not zits
Not pustules
Not exactly
Just—sores or
Pests, reminders of age—
Of endless rest

The Ghost

When we got old my cousin said,
Very matter-of-factly
She said, she said exactly—
Not exactly
She told me a story, but
"Well," she said, because she didn't know if it was true
She had no way of knowing
Because by then everyone had turned to glue
Though
It happened (my cousin said) in the shower
With Mom
(her mother, my aunt)
(she too had turned to dew)
And he had an erection
Who? I said
Grandpa (she said)

In the shower
They were showering together
When Mom was a little girl
At the angle of his little curl
Which curled up
Into her face
She saw it
She can't erase it (my cousin said)
She never could erase it from her mind

I saw it too (but I didn't say)
My story was by then passe,

But I saw it too
The circumcised penis of
A circumcised Jew
He and me
Nothing happened
Just a shower
Water

Soap
A rough towel on my head
Pajamas
Teeth
Sleep well and to bed.

Twins

One of us was meant to die
To be eaten alive
It was supposed to be me.

But I rebelled
Hell no
My insides rotting
May never be clean
But I would–I would—be seen.

Or not.
Not it seems
The end of all our dreams
When instead of me
It's my brother who died

But only inside
Where his soul should be
Where his self has been
Devoured by kin.

He breathes—
He walks—
He phones—
His life atones
Like a Cohen,
Forbidden from touching the
Dead
Or their bones.

Immortality

They slit you open with a poultry knife
And fished me out with rope
Into the June night
Where there was no sense of sight
Just men, with glasses and antiseptic soap
For the endoscope

The Holy Land

Uncle Milton Way
In Jerusalem
I remember him
My father's favorite fairy friend
From the olden days
The good old days
The golden days
Baltimore!

Where men were men
And Jews were really Jews
Jews in leather, in leather shoes
And brimmed men's hats
And spats

Our men
Fought so bravely
To defeat the Nazi foe
Hitler and his blunt mustache
Dead Jews all in a row

But on Uncle Milton Way
In Jerusalem, in August,
We are robust
It is bright day
Nothing to fear
Not Hezbollah—
Isis, Isil, Taliban
Al-Qaeda
Vey es mir!

Here are
Men with beards
Babies and dogs and kids on
Roller blades
And lovers wearing
Baseball caps

No bowlers
Not here
There.
Where men were really men
And Jews knew how to pray
Shaharit at day
Mincha midway
Ma-ariv, eve's offering
Where Jews were really Jews

Uncle Milton in Orthodox attitude
He was my dad's favorite (fairly fairy) friend
We kids intuited, we knew, it was
Sort of
Obvious

Fussy little man
With precision bow ties
Pitty-pat
Purring sighs
Precisely arranged and beautiful things
But no wedding ring
No signs of lust, lost or lingering–

He loved the Opera
Verdi
Puccini's *Turando.*

In the Jewelry Museum

Young couple devouring each other
On the bench across from me
Underground on the Number Three

Me, on my way to the Metropolitan Museum
To see
Ancient jewels
Ancient jewelry—

She's lovely, dark and dainty even
Lips, cheek bones, that pointy chin
With blue black blood in her ancestry
(genes, I think)
He's covered with zits
He covers her with kisses
All over her face, here and here and here
Does she like it, the way he sucks on her
With his pressing pink lips?
Resist! Resist!

She smiles from behind
His big hair,
His wild head
While I take furtive glances
His zits are red

His insistence
Her more common sense
Or sensibility
I don't know
I can't tell.

When I was her age,
About her age, that is,
I was on the subway,
Jazz and jizz–
Naïve, obscured,

A girl from the suburbs
When a man
Came from behind me
And rubbed himself
Into a tent pole,
A tree
I didn't know or notice though
When my friends saw, and, giggling, said:
Oh! Ooh!
He's rubbing himself on you.
I didn't even really know
Abashed, embarrassed, rather than ashamed
While he, aflamed, affianced in me,
Glowed in the dark.

As we exited into Central Park
To smoke a joint
Or do some blow–
Which is what we did then––
The grownups didn't know––
Because there were no grownups way back when
Just big children, empty smiles and empty men
Men who made money
And brought home the bacon
For us un-benighted and godforsaken
At home––

I got off at 72nd Street
The Upper West Side alight in light sleet
Enormous old buildings with antique insides
And me in my good cloth coat, dark blue
My solid black leather shoes,
Middle aged and respectable and–
Correct in every way
Maternal, married, safe–
No longer *treyf*
The slim gold wedding band
And slim gold watch
Walking east towards art

While underneath and underfoot
Floating, liquid, all that mess of
Love and sex and *yuck* and *gross*
Youth is overdose.

I was far from the museum.
I no longer even wanted to go
Across the park to see
Sparkling jewels, ancient jewelry
Of ancient long-dead V.I.Ps
Gone, without names
Again and anon
Frozen in crystal and tacky
By my own good taste
Expensive, bought from a store
Gloating, an eyesore
Young love on the shelf, forever more

That's what we thought, about love—
That's what we thought we knew
When really all we knew were their jewels—
Diadems
Crowns
Bracelets and rings
Golden gold beaten into beautiful things
And delicate shapes
Miniature elephants
Darling dancing apes
Strawberries and grapes
Lions, butterflies, birds
Flowers, of course—lots and lots of flowers
Made of hours
And days and weeks and years
And eons–
Always the eons
Flowers made of ruby and jade
Alert and gorgeous
Unfaded, unfazed–

Unlike their dead former owners
Long gone to dust and
Seed and stone.

And yet—to own such jewels!
How fine!
How divine!

Going to the Shops

So many pretty things to see
To charm the eye
Egg-blue door
Gray velvet sky

Twinkle twinkle pretty gem
Behind plate glass thickness
A diadem,
Defying sickness—
Fever, phlegm

For a full year before my wedding
My mother worried
About the weather
What if?
What if it rained?

The weather, that day
Was perfect
In all the photo books
There are smiles on the
Faces of dust and ashes.

Crusaders

Those illuminated manuscripts
We studied
Poured over
In the sixth grade
Eleven and 12-year-olds

Deep magical blue and golds,
Angels, monkeys, monks
Doing their careful Medieval work,
Their workmanship,
Their exquisite craft
In the Medieval cold
The Medieval dark

And I, a Jew, a weird girl
With wild hair
And bloody knees
I was seized by desire
To please, God—
Let me, too
Make such beautiful gorgeous things
Make me enraptured

Captured
By that shimmering fragile beauty

In
Those manuscripts.

The Wedding

Because here we are dancing:
Come Asher come Jacob
But here we are dancing:
In circles and couples
And here we are dancing:
The sky outside purple
The beams on the stone walls
The echo of ages—
The wailing of heartbreak
The heartbreak of blood—
Of blood spilled and blood blotting
The ground all beneath us
The ground that's been trodden
With horses and armies
With camels and pilgrims
With longing for anguish
With dreams of delusion
And searing for prophets.

And the desert lies flatly
Its seasons of seething—
While we, we are dancing:
Our darling among us
Our darling, his darling
Just come from the chuppah
Behind him the dead from
Last week's many dying.

But now! Such rejoicing
Our heads filled with wonder
The city all splendor
The sky's starry sparkling
While we keep on dancing
In Hebrew's joy pacing
Our prayers in our swaying
Revelations! He lives.

Holy Sonnets

When you open up your veins to
God
And ask Him in—
What then?

If He agrees
To flow in your cells
Bright blue tubes—
What flows through?

Is that how Bach became?
And countless nameless saints
And monks
And rabbis, scholars—ragged holy men?
What about them?

And what about the end?
The when?
When blood stops
When the beat of breath ceases?
When increases are null and void?

The ride—
Over

The vast nothing
The endless huffing
Of the universe—
While in the hearse—
A celluloid

The Chinese Lady with the Chinese Eyes

My grandfather
Was always tense,
always ready to blow
Impatient and O.C.D.
He couldn't see
The good in me
Twinned, as I was
To my somewhat younger brother
My junior by a year and change

The room where we slept
Charged and strange
Those Chinese eyes staring black on the two of us
As we
Age four, age three,
Or more—
Tore fast and heedless down
Our grandparents' apartment hall
The parquet floor,
The parakeet,
Grown-up feet
Coming fast and faster
Towards the disaster

We were, and we made
We were so afraid
Of those defiant sparkling Chinese eyes

A surprise, then,
When,
After both of them were buried and gone
The house and lawn
Where our parents grew to grownup growth
A memory—
From another century
Our grandparents by then were ghosts

And my favorite cousin
My father's sister's second son—
Hung
That same Chinese lady's Chinese face
In the empty entry space
Wide and sunny
Pleasant, non-showy
Of his suburban Boston home

Where she shone
In newness
No longer alone
In the dull gloom
Of that back room

Ectasis

John Donne wrote holy sonnets
Nineteen in all
I learned in the fall
Of my senior year

Above and below
Huff and blow
A love poem, about God
Darling good Jesus, suffering on his tree
The poet's desire
To put his soul to the fire

But not to die
Not like we Jews:
Burned at the stake
For God's holy sake

Senior year—
When I lost my cherry
To some extremely very
horny hound

another kid, my age, more or less,
No sweet slow caress
The sound of him
Moving over me
Grunting
While over head
All that bunting
Go Saxons!

Another football season.
While me, in my skivvies,
Committed treason.

Though come to think of it. . .

Perhaps it wasn't his upright outright member
But his urgent finger fingering me,
Splitting me into two, but no—
It was more than two, it was more like—
Endlessly

It was only later,
When I'd left home
For college
And all that verse came
Collapsing, again, into my ears
All my nightmares
All my fears
Come true
It was as they had said.
Rapture—a deathbed

Bird

The woman with her hymn,
Her husband, a homonym,
Forever more, inviting in—

She got him with her scissored self,
Her splay of legs, her oozing wealth
Pretty precision on the shelf

Her light on dim
She, elegant, slim,
Like a seabird: scales, fin—

Flashing there, bright and skim,
Her lips and thighs an urgent whim,
Bring her to the very rim–

Now diving down and downward plunging
All her sins and his expunging
Enfolding him, torpid, lunging

And flapping upwards, bright liquid blue
Endless sky and endless you
my love, goodbye, goodbye, adieu

Because hers was radiant, a lilting lift–
While you churn and burn and sift
She soared off above the cliffs

The Bride

She dazzled
Big teeth
Huge grin
Dark and slim
In flashing tennis whites
Velvet nights
On Lino floor
In the arms of fine slim
Ivy men

Say when
Say when
And always yes

What a mess
A bad trade
The Negro maid
In matching uniforms
Of pale green or pink
Notwithstanding
Her own mother's reprimanding
Motherhood was crushing
Demanding
More of her than the drink
At night helped to quiet
The daily riot
Of unruly things with farts and curls
Her mink
Her strand of pearls

The girls for doubles:
And then perhaps
We'll talk of our troubles

Boyfriends

Did I mention suicide?
Three old boyfriends, three in a row
Three dead ducks
It happened
—a while ago

When we were full of sex
When we were made of sex
Of that tingle jingle in the jungle
The hunger
The unrepentant, unremitting rub-a-dub-dub
Puppies, cub, pubes and hair—there and there
Where it tangled into tangles of a wiry revolt

The first: by his own hand
His neurological connectors a joke
Light a match
Poof!
up in smoke
His mommy, his daddy,
In their big modern house in the Hollywood Hills
His stinking charred body on the sill.

For thirty years, she called me—
His mother did
On the day he died, she called me to say
Oh
by the way—
This
That
Her second son
Of the three of them the golden one
The one who was meant to be—
(Fill in the blank, his future was brighter than pulsating light)

He and I tangling on the guest bed
In the room off the garage which
Itself was so clean you could throw a dinner party there
Near the guest room down three short flights of stairs

Number Two had blue eyes
Crystal blue
And a wide mouth
and he, too, was slated for a future so dazzling—
it was guaranteed
look at me! notice me!
The girls
flocked to him

I offered up my body
My being
My virginity, for what it was worth
And (of course)
My adoration.

But.
It was not his will
To remain
Poof! He was off

What were we?
I'll tell you what we were:
Disappointed
And then one day
He took his own life
With pills and a knife

The third
My very first and very best love
Predating sex and lust,
He was: simply: always there
A teddy bear
Like light, like air
Under my covers late at night
Pillow fight!
I dare you with all my might
Will you catch it?
Will you dare?

He caught it, all right
He found the light
He found the endless soul's delight
Of destruction and death and sex and meth
And crushed jagged jangles inside your veins
Never mind
He's fine
Not dead at all
Just in thrall.

Ropes

My hands were 7,
Or 17
Perhaps as old as——but no more than--thirty

But never this,
No, not these spotted
Whorls and blue bumps,
These moles and throbbing ropes of veiny
Worms, flirty
Blue worms threading beneath the skin

The sin
Is not dying
Not when I had the chance
Chemotherapy kept me here
They lanced me with needles and filled me with fumes.
Rooms filled with the slow drip drip drip–

Of——well, it kind of looks like vodka, with vodka's viscous sheen
I was keen not to die
Life---it looms--wrathful
An Alcmene

Domesticity

Lay the supper table
With pretty things:
The faded flowered cloth with its tattered pink ground
That your grown daughter didn't want to keep
It was out of kilter, no longer in fashion or perhaps
The wrong shape
It didn't drape
Properly for her though for me
It is lovely, something rare and pure
Like the brief flowering of April—
Here—and then
Until next year

To put a pot of roses at the center
A pot of miniature roses that someone left as a
gift
For the weekend spent at the rift
Of the world where the lake meets the sky
And it sat dead and dry and lifeless
Until, quite without warning,
It turned green and sprouted anew again—
In early April. On its own, without water or care
It plunged upwards into the air—

Knives and forks, folded patterned napkins made of
Cloth
Old soft cotton, well used, cast-off
By that same faceless nameless who-knows-who?
Someone who didn't want the old-fashioned hues
And over soft fibers and faded yesterdays
And long forgotten disappointment
A million maybes
A million we'll sees—
Of April, that month of glory, gone again–

Until next year
We can only hope
For next year to be here
And when
And when

Tishrei

I am greedy with weather.
For days that snap with wind
Or fire the eye
With color:
Red, orange, and the smell of fallen apples
With brown splotches where the worms have dined
As well as others of their kind
The prancing, nervous, elegant fawn
With its mother
Approaching tenderly at dawn
For a snack on the
Backyard apple trees
That drop their fruit:
It's gravity you see—
the hum of humming bees
Of late summer and on into full blown autumnal bliss
Ah! To hold on to all this
Just to think—
How I might greedily drink to drunkenness.
My confession:
I will eat, suck, swill, chew, and breathe it into me
I will get my fill
And more—
As the sun climbs up and through its daily dome
Of blue, mauve, golden pink
I will drink and drink and drink until
It's time to pay the final bill.

Kohelet

When you cleave open your organs and say:
Bleed in me
Let my blood be Thine
What then?
Even Shakespeare died
Is dead
His bones somewhere
Or maybe not
Maybe already gone to mud and clay
The daily turning of the—day

It doesn't matter
Shakespeare is dead. Tolstoy; Dickens: Henry James
Six feet under
A casket of names–books on the shelf
The former self—
No more

Jesus Christ is long gone
Moses
Maimonides
The Rambam. The Baal Shem Tov
Einstein and Bach:
Gone gone gone!

For others—for others whose flesh melts and mourns
The diurnal passing of
Weather, stars, worms

Kohelet his real (Hebrew) name
His bleakness his fame
How dare he?
How awful!
That awful bleat of death
And useless uselessness
And yet:
Hold fast to God!

Hold fast, he said!

. . . . it's my favorite book
Of the Hebrew bible
Some of it a weird, long snooze:
They piss off the boss
And never learn
No—not then, not later, and certainly not now
A quarrelsome lot, my people, my Jews

The Slave

The pills neatly labelled
and swaddled in plastic
So dear–so close–
To live and die,
An ecclesiastic

The Pact

The marriage bed:
The wedding presents
Two sets of dishes
Charming and pleasant.

The child's cradle:
The baby inside,
The soft smell of powder,
The days long and wide.

The marriage bed:
A queen for the day,
The newly soft pouching of—
The family way.

The crib in the room
With the wall-to-wall carpet:
The wailing of children,
The trip to the market.

The marriage bed:
Tumble and writhe.
You're alone and befriended.
Time with its scythe.

The marriage bed:
The habit of lust
Time fleeing backwards
Like an animal, trussed.

The marriage bed:
Fresh sheets changed weekly.
The mislaid word
Sideways or obliquely.

The crib in the corner:
Of the room down the hall
Where did you mislay it?
Time used to crawl.

The marriage bed:
The children all grown
The husband beside you
Beside him and alone.

The marriage bed:
The years of time
The family collection
A paradigm.

New Jersey in Winter

The green sofa was white
With its sprinkling of pillows
Yellow, bright,
Recovered in velvet, (your taste has changed)
And plumped to perfection
And rearranged

On the table before it,
(the one from upstate)
An arrangement of flowers
In the jug: ejaculate
A fission of sunbeams
A fistful of fate

The rug–all vegetable dyes
Imported from Turkey
And suburbanized.
The lovely surroundings—
The sweet surrounds–
Of winter in quietude.
Parks and playgrounds

The hiss of the heaters
The itch in your crotch
Your heart, how it teeters
As moon and stars watch
Your heart how it scurries
Your heart scabbing over:
That dear violet swatch!

The patterning of violets
Against a field of green grass—

A field of green grasses
Blue breath of no less
Then violets and roses
Chinoiserie, plumaged parrots—

Life lived on its merits.
With buckets of proses.

And tumbled in dreams with–
Purpose and poses.

Death of the Poet

The smell of the forest
The sound of the sea
The salt on your kisses
The skin on your knee
The skin on your forehead
The red on your cheek
The rough, the delicious
The sheen on the creek

Nature, her bounty,
Was her bounty as well
It was more than the patterns
Of seaweed and shell
And scatter of deer scat
And drop of pinecone
On forest floor or path
Through deep loam

Her bones white and brittle
Inside a scorned sheath
Like the poems she gave birth to—
Enshrined underneath

Latitude and Longitude

Inside–
In the dark tangle of guts
Of viscera
Blood and muscle and brain
A million billion miles
Of that brought forth
In pain

The hidden and beating
The impossible! —life
Made of blots-- invisible
And planetary strife
Of endless non-being
The nothing, un-space
The zero conundrum
The moment of grace

Discernment

What Is Real

The branch at the window
The yellow house on the corner
The smell of your baby's skin
Oxygen and sin

What Maybe Isn't So Real

The stories you've read in the Bible
Hints and promises of—
That lover–you remember his kisses
August, September, near misses

What Is Not Real

That in high school you were what you were
The way she looked in the film
If it's meant to be, it will be
If it's chemical, it's chemistry

New

When you're very young
 You don't think
  I'm fresh off the line
   I just got here
A seedling–

You don't think at all
 It's just there
 It just is
  Your life like a dare
The trees and the air–

The swing
 In the park
  The blue of the sky
   the hug of warm dark
a now, not a why——

The non-thing of time
 Or the passing of hours
 The rain on the window
  The leaves on the bower
Are green——

Hoarders

My mother-in-law: Lola
Loved Pappagallo shoes
Lined up in their original boxes
Bedded down with rustling white tissue
Clean and crisp, smelling of expensive things
Of department stores that no longer exist
Ladies' lunches, talcum powder, fittings,
Arranged side by side on the built-in shelving
of her walk-in closet in Philadelphia
where after she was widowed—
and sold the family home—
(the one with the backyard swimming pool
The basement catacomb)
She lived in her widow's splendid sunny
Eleventh-floor flat
Filled with this and that
(a lot of this and that)
French reproduction antiques
Covered in appliqué and arranged
Around the room were also
Large African figurines and crystal vases
And heavily framed oil paintings from France (and elsewhere)
The candy-dishes, the double-chair,
The soft plush beige and brown carpeting
Good for grandchildren, good for crawling
Around on tender tiny knees–

And then they grew up and she grew old
And all that was left were the dregs and the mold
And the things once loved that were no longer wanted
And the things so dearly cared for we now taunted
And in her closet—sarcophagi for shoes
And under the pines, the pine box for Jews.

Grownups

We took our cues from our parents
They lived in a disappeared world
It never existed. It wasn't ever real.
It was a thought—
Thought up by someone else, by other people
It had its own smell.
Its own pulse
It lived on a shelf.

We were children and had no choice.
It was a case of or-else
It was the chase for clean underpants
Television.
It was noise,
Unnecessary and unrepentant
Unseeing and resplendent

Jephthah's Daughter

I dwell in the house
(Some house)
Shelling peas, beating flax
My body for others, soft as dough
Molten wax
To emerge into flashing sun's desert brilliance
I will live in the pages of my deathly resilience

Tourists

We flew across the globe
To land in Nepal.
The mass of people
Selling things:
Trinkets mainly
Authentic Nepalese tribal art
Made in China

We climbed a mountain
To Tiger's Nest
An ancient Buddhist monastery
Where along the hair-turn path up up up
Teenage girls ran in flip flops
To their jobs scrubbing toilets
At the top of the stairs
Where at last I too climbed
My bladder bursting
With urgency

And the small fee to pee
In a filthy corner perfumed with
The humidity of a thousand thousand foreign bladders
And large intestines churning forth the
Spicy vegetarian food

I was in no mood
For all those gods
Some with hundreds of arms
And elephant eyes
Made of crimson dyes

I am a Jew
I do not comprehend.
I cannot fathom
I fail; a failure of the imagination
The spirit of the divine in you
Meets the divine in me

All I could think about
Was my urgency
That bladder; that bowl
That stomach churning
Again and afoul
Of all that is holy and good and true

I am a Jewish Jew
And happy to be home (at last)
In suburban New Jersey:
My house with plumbing
The cherry trees laced as they do
In April and then into May
All that gold and yellow spray

The Airport

I no longer belong here
In this place of push and push
Burritos, pizza, excess grub
And noise from speakers hidden
In secret slits in secret vents.

It is not the girls in hot pink tight pants
With spreading wide thighs and every fold
And careful fold a rant.
It's not the pink sun burn
Of flapping bellies bulging.

It's none of that.
(Though I, disturbed
And with the bones of a bird
Feel my inside innards contract:
Oh, the injury, the injury!)

No: it's the fist
This endless dirge.
Take her, she's yours

Diaspora

Where does a Jew belong?
A Jewy Jew with Jewish skin
(with greenish owlish Mediterranean tones:
Olive, yellow, banker's loans)
And kosher-keeping: gills and fins
And why? Why keep the ancient
Whirling can-not commands
Of an ancient bloody desert tribe?
A people doomed to suicide.
(By hands other than our own
Crying: blood suckers, loan-sharking,
parasitical fat and hawk like bone)

And then---Jersusalem.
City of white stone.
Of desert light and desert
Sand-blowing in a fine soft
Annoying grit
(impossible to get rid of it)

The all of dreams and a dream made flesh
The biblical tongue, the aromatic
Mesh of jasmine-scented
Spice filled streets and winding
Alleys and Arabs—their impossible mumble
(Talk about babble, talk about jargon!)
The daily binding
Of phylacteries

How good to live in desert's fractured blister

And scattered we go, the children of the
Children of the children who crossed over
Deep dark churning waters.
Our grandmothers, our grandfathers—

And me and mine in
A lovely old house on a
Shaded street—
Old growth trees
Grandmother's dishes (delicate with pink trim)
Grandfather's stately old chest of drawers
(stately, simple, of burnished old wood
You can't buy them like that anymore)
And other solid pleasant things
That generations of perseverance buy

Why would I leave it?
Why would I?

The Holy Trinity

Dr. Berman was my first
I lay on his breaded sofa:
Liverwurst
Shining with dreams and sobbing
With brother, with father
My nipples, scared, stood up
My blood burned in my acid belly
The smell of my own sour breath

While his slow breathing behind me
Like a cushioned buffer
Broken only by his caution:
Don't look back but see—
Above!
The black ink drawings of pure sweet love
A mother holding her baby to her breast
A child in his child's bed
The black ink drawings framed in black
Her future, with husband, and on her back
She will receive his gifts of sperm
The swelling belly and milky breasts
That was my future
It was no joke
It was the best possible future for girls like her
Pretty, educated, fucked up, demure
Don't look behind the shining door
Suicide is such a bore

Dr. Abrams on the upper east side
Ushered me in, a sacred bride
I was a bride bristling with wrath
And horror, like a mangled toad or like Sylvia Plath
The patient (me) on the couch withered and mad
Though not so mad as a raving whore
The death of self is such a bore

My third, a German, Dr. Jensen:
To her I came as if to advent
The season of: believe in me
What is it that I do not see
Is it so terrible to strive, to be
And she: listening, maternal, with her
Soothing green love seat
Her hair, her voice, her hands and feet
Tucked and docile, steady, sure
Your psyche is yours to explore
Self-destruction, such a bore

When God (at last) appeared He said:
What's blue is blue what's red is red
What comes will go. What's goes is gone.
Dandelions in a plush green lawn

Gray white haloes of floating seed
That float away Not gone: freed

After Infection

The white house
With the orange door
A thing you didn't see before
An orange door.

The color of a tangerine
Salt-water taffy
Margarine.
A magazine version
In a magazine world
With taffy-hued tulips
Domestic perfection
A string of pearls

The field of daffodils
In a field of cut green
Grass smelling of
Things unknown and unseen.
But the tulips, red and open.
Vaginal, obscene

The creep of the vinca
The budding of cherry
The fragrance of pink blossom
And shower of white petals
A velvety soft snow of April
In all its begetting

In the Yeats House

You just keep dying
Over and over
You won't quit
How tiresome it is
How you re-enact the final act
Over and over without a moment's cease.
The suicide to launch a thousand books
To launch a thousand launches

With your boiling skull in the gray black sea
Your roots dangling in the naked air

How tedious is
your ceaseless suicide

And readers who don't read
But merely plead: please let us watch
And gawk as you kill and stalk

The Wonderful Thing

The bicycle is a wonderful invention
A whirligig
The pedals—
And
The smell of metallic salt
Just two wheels, spoked
And tender, strong with rubber

My best beloved
Loved to ride.
St. Francisville—the great deep gloom.
Forests sticky and wet and freighted
With bright birds.
There, on the side of the road that
Had no sides,
A car came by
and she was gone

Later, and crazed with fear
Of thugs unleashed
I whirled down a hill.
It was like flying,
Light and weightless—
On my bike I flew
On my bike I felt again
The flash of my own kinetic sin—
I do, I do

The Blink

I'm afraid I'll forget it
I want it to stay
Paper and pen,
Paper and pen

I want to remember it
The color of tulips
A retina sun burst
Blood on my hand

The burst in the heart
Like the love of a child
Like the love of a dog.
Sweet puppy, come see

It's never tomorrow
It's always–explain.
The incomprehensible
My brain hurts from thinking it
The moment.
The blink

Hands

When I see my hands
Stretched out
On piano keys
Or chopping: something:
Carrots
Zucchini for zucchini bread
The growth of someone else's garden

Len poco pui andante

Sleep, sleep, my child—

They are my mother's hands—
In front of me

Schlaf—

And back and back and all the way back
Under the ground
The mothers mourn my spotted hands

Virginia

I roamed
In the woods
I was alone there
In the woods I was alone
The river churned
I was alone
The sky burned
I was alone
In the woods I learned:
Dear God
Take me and–
Make me Yours

Last Night I Dreamed a Gospel Song

. . . I could hear it in my veins.
Its tune was—
Soaring

Words came too
Words of praise
Of joy

Clapping and stamping

It was wondrous; I wanted to record it

When I woke, it was still playing.
I could hear it in my ears.
I caught the tune, the refrain

It was enough,
Enough to start
Enough to write down
In scribbles on scrap paper
By my bedside lamp
Next to my alarm clock

Shall I sing it for you?

The Art Collector

Daddy refused to die
He bought things—
A Rembrandt (it was very small)
Hanging in the entry hall
A flat in Tel Aviv
  With marble stairs
        Flowering trees
              A swimming pool
                    The Mediterranean Sea

The house in Georgetown
Picasso, Matisse–
A private jet for eight for lease
(come see he said, come see my things)
Paintings from the paintings store
  A blue Aubusson for the floor
      The garden rich with vine and bloom
          I'm going no where nowhere soon.

Europe

In the Museum of God:
There are:
Charred bones
And other Sapiens remains
Bling and stains
Jewels and veins
But mainly only and essentially this
Blink once blink twice
And you miss

Portugal

I hate Your
Holy places
Your high domed rooms hung
With your dead son
Lined with gold
Rhinestone jewels
Adorning haloed human saints
(Some saints, how they murdered themselves)
The adoring throng
The chants, the song
The lapis lazuli tiled floors
The dead the dead the dead by scores
A million sore and suppurating human bones
The blood spilled
The right wronged
While we, in dark corners by candlelight
Bless bread
In ancient tongue

To incline our natures to cleave to—
The Holy One

Atonement

Weather makes a difference:
Heavy wet air like a witch's kiss
Cold streaks—wet bullets of misery
Like a greasy pot you can't scrub clean
Overgrown vines strangling a fence.

Weather makes a difference:
Bright blue June and emerald grass
Butterflies dancing with bees
Don't sting me, bees, I'm your friend.

Weather makes a difference:
We were all so young then
Dancing down the lane
Walking from the yellow school bus
To our mothers
Who were waiting for us in the kitchen with a snack
And all outside blue and black.

Weather makes a difference:
Blue sky black tar black limbs
Orange and red leaves singing their farewells—
Leaves falling on our heads
We didn't know what made that pleased and happy smell
We thought it was autumn.

Weather makes a difference and—
We did not know that that wonderful aroma
Of falling leaves.
Of crisp blue air
Was the smell of decay.

We did not know who would walk
And who would fall away.

Shabbat

On Shabbos I like to garden
(*shabbos goy,
 Shabbos goy)
A Jews who likes to garden
The garden, a sanctuary
Where I daven
The prayer of the Holy One
Is dirt beneath my nails and ragged edges
Worn and uneven:

Oi what a mess.

As I work
With spade and shears
Weed and trim
Crying out all aloud to Him:

Dear God in Your heaven
Forgive my sin
As I, a Jew
Born to Jewish mother
Under the cover of
Sky and cloud

Cry aloud or in my
Heart
Just let me be a tool
for your Art—

1977

I do, I do
Remember the all of you
Your bright blue ocean blue sky blue eyes
Your high cheekbones
your fake Irish lilt—
And your preference for a certain rich red wine
Which to this day makes me revive
Your high-arched perfect feet
And expressive toes, your curved calf muscles
Your poem, published in the college journal,
About a sliver of soap
Melting on a lover's thigh
In the shared shower
Under the eaves
Of the third floor college house
On the edge of the tennis courts
Where on warm days student athletes wacked away
At *thwack, thwack, thwack*
While you and I lay in each other's otherness
Amazed and entranced
In sex but it was more than sex
It was the disappearance of self
The blending of boundaries into the other
The bliss of non-
Being except better than that too because we were so young and so new

Forty years later I heard of your death
The bullet to the brain
The confession of pain unceasing
Your siblings—there were so many of them—
How they mourned you
But none so much as I
Who, left behind, at nineteen,
Left for some better version of lips and eyes,
Raged: why?

I mourned and cried and gasped for air
I choked on my fury, my endless abandoned state
The fate of those not deemed sufficiently excellent
And so I rent my face and tore my soul
And didn't know you—
We were not friends—
We did not write Christmas cards–
Or trade photos of the children
Or of vacations on the beach or in the mountains

But instead, there was nothing
For years of it, then decades,
And then on that day I learned of your brutality
Your self-murder, your death by depression or–
Soul death before death
Or lack of love or hope or faith or Christ
What do I know?
Your brain sliced and shattered
Into a million bloody shards

Later you sent me a message–
I think you sent me a message—
It was on a license plate on a car
In the parking lot at the Whole Foods
In my town where I'd gone to get expensive fresh fish
And the license plate said only this:
Wherever you are

Jennifer Anne Moses is the author of seven books of fiction and non-fiction, including *Bagels and Grits: A Jew on the Bayou*, *Visiting Hours*, and *The Man Who Loved His Wife*. *Domesticity* is her first published collection of poetry. She is also a painter. She and her husband are the parents of three grown children, and live in Montclair, New Jersey. www.jenniferannemosesarts.com

www.ingramcontent.com/pod-product-compliance
Lightning Source LLC
Chambersburg PA
CBHW022009100426
42736CB00041B/1344